My Will,
God's Response
God's Will,
My Response

*May God bless you
as you take this
walk with me.*

Noges

12·12·21

My Will,
God's Response
God's Will,
My Response

A MEMOIR OF LOSING A LOVED ONE

Aletha **Voges**

TATE PUBLISHING *& Enterprises*

Published by Tate Publishing & Enterprises, LLC
127 E. Trade Center Terrace | Mustang, Oklahoma 73064 USA
1.888.361.9473 | www.tatepublishing.com

Tate Publishing is committed to excellence in the publishing industry. The company reflects the philosophy established by the founders, based on Psalm 68:11,
"The Lord gave the word and great was the company of those who published it."

Published in the United States of America

ISBN: 978-1-61566-269-2
1. Biography & Autobiography / Religious
2. Family & Relationships / Death, Grief, Bereavement
09.12.09

Dedication

From my experience, the greatest spiritual growth comes amid the greatest personal struggles. In the sixteen months that my husband, Ethan, fought his battle with cancer involving his liver and pancreas, God became my rock and my fortress.

Ethan was a pastor of churches in Adair and Arcadia, Iowa, and Klamath Falls, Oregon, before following his heart and accepting an appointment as chaplain with the United States Army in 1973. He served at Fort Gordon, Georgia; Korea (unaccompanied); Fort Carson, Colorado; Baumholder, Germany; Fort Monroe, Virginia; Fort Richardson, Alaska; and Sharp Army Depot, Stockton, and The Defense Language Institute in Monterey, California. He retired from the army in 1993 and served as pastor at St. Mark's Lutheran Church in Sunnyvale, California. The lure of chaplaincy ministry brought him to Seattle, Washington, in December of 1997, where he served as chaplain for Lutheran Ministries Seattle, specializing in ministering to veterans. Ethan retired a second time in 2003 and continued to preach several times a month for pastors needing a Sunday replacement. He also began a ministry to churches with vacancies.

While in Seattle, Ethan developed a special relationship as a mentor to a young teenager who found himself in juvenile detention for taking part in a murder. He faithfully visited this young teen weekly, and when he was moved 150 miles away, he visited monthly. From his ministry to the young teen, he only retired when his health no longer permitted the trips.

Dining out brought enjoyment to Ethan, and he was happiest when he could treat someone to a meal. At military functions, he sought out the lone soldier who needed company. Ethan thought of others' needs and did what he could to help.

Ethan thoroughly enjoyed driving, and we visited all fifty states. With our five children scattered across the United States, traveling seven thousand miles in less than three weeks was not unusual.

In our travels, we experienced the beauty of our country that God has created for us to enjoy.

In July of 2004, Ethan and I flew to Germany with our oldest son, Nathan, as our tour guide. There we were able to meet Ethan's third cousin and other German relatives. We also toured Berlin and Leipzig, as well as many smaller cities. Visiting castles required climbing hundreds of steps. Cities are conducive to walking, and we put many kilometers on our shoes. In December, we traveled to Los Angeles to spend a few days with our son Brian and his family at Disneyland. As I look back on these vigorous and enjoyable trips, I can now recognize signs that Ethan was beginning to lose the spark in his step.

In this book I attempt to share the struggles we encountered as we took this journey with the Lord and the lessons I learned amidst the pain and sorrow. My prayer is that our Lord and Savior Jesus Christ might also touch your life as you read these pages and as you walk with me through the struggles and sorrow to understanding and peace.

To that end, I dedicate this book to my beloved husband,

Chaplain Ethan Carl Voges
1939–2006

Thanks

God created this book through me. He orches-
trated the events of our lives, he opened my eyes
to see his blessings around us daily, and he gave
me the words of this book. I can only kneel in awe
at his love for us. Praise and thanks be to him!

I also want to thank my sister, Rhoda. Without
her constant support and prayerful encouragement, my journey would have been more difficult.
Three times she traveled from North Carolina to
Washington to be at my side when I needed her.
She has been my inspiration and proofreader. I
have been blessed to have a wonderful sister like
her. Praise and thanks to God!

Thanks are due to Kristi Galindo Dyson, who
walked beside me during some very tough days. She
was always a phone call away. Praise and thanks to
God for her prayerful support. Thank you, Dian

Colasurdo, for your help in proofing this book, for your encouragement as I put this work together, and for walking with me when I needed a friend. Thank you, God, for placing these women in my life.

The faithful support of each of our children and their families brought us comfort and were there for us when we needed someone. Thank you Nathan, Nannette (Nan), Brian, Timothy, and Philip, for your love and care for us. I give God thanks for my brother, Clifford, and his wife, Peggy, for dear friends Ed and Ruby, and for all who helped in so many ways. If I listed every name, this book would never end. All praise and thanks to God for their love!

Thanks are due to all the people on my e-mail list and their extended influence, who prayed diligently for Ethan and me during the long months of our journey through pain, doubt, and uncertainty to strength, understanding, and peace. Praise and thanks to God!

Table of Contents

God's Plan: Our Response

In the fall of 2004, the northwest district of the Lutheran Church Missouri Synod called Ethan to consider temporary pastoral leadership in one of two churches in the district. The first was a small church in eastern Idaho near the Grand Teton Mountains. The second was a larger church in the city of Yakima in central Washington. After much consideration, Ethan decided he could use his gifts at either church and asked the district to decide where he was needed most. Ethan received a phone call from the church in Yakima asking him to become their vacancy pastor.

God was already at work fulfilling his plan. Ethan began working in Yakima on Thanksgiving. Traveling back and forth on I-90 across Snoqualmie Pass during the winter can be difficult. Armed with his snow shovel and chains, he would leave our home in Kent on Saturday to drive to Yakima and return each Thursday afternoon. Had Ethan been serving the church in Idaho, he would not have been coming home regularly, and I would not have noticed how jaundiced he was becoming. He very quickly could have been so ill that medical treatment would not have been possible.

Think about your life and the decisions you have made. Can you see the hand of God directing you to make certain decisions? Did you choose a wrong path? How has God used that path for his glory?

Lord, we do not know how our actions and decisions of today will affect our future. You can see our yesterdays, our today, and our tomorrows. We pray that our will may be in tune with your will and that we would walk the path of blessing you have prepared for us. Amen.

_____

_____

_____

_____

_____

_____

_____

_____

_____

MY WILL, GOD'S RESPONSE: GOD'S WILL, MY RESPONSE

Surrender

On February 1, 2005, I was preparing to lead a Bible study about peace for our Lutheran Women's Missionary League (LWML) Circle. One of the passages was: "The mind of sinful man is death, but the mind controlled by the Spirit is life and peace" (Romans 8:6).

I asked myself, "How does one's mind become controlled by the Spirit?" Immediately I felt God answer me, "Surrender." And so I surrendered my life to God to use as he saw fit. Little did I know how this decision would affect my life during the next fifteen months.

On Thursday January 26, 2005, Ethan had come home looking very jaundiced. I took him to the doctor on Friday, where he had blood work done. He went back to Yakima that week, and on the afternoon of Wednesday, February 2, I received a call from the clinic saying Ethan needed to have a fasting ultrasound done ASAP. Since he was coming home on Thursday, I scheduled the procedure for Friday morning, February 4. After the procedure, we had breakfast. Because he was itching from the high levels of toxins in his body, and I did not know how to relieve it, I convinced him to see a doctor to get some relief.

The doctor referred us to the gastroenterologists (GI) who told him to remain in the clinic and not to leave for six hours; they needed an empty stomach to place a stent into the duct at the head of the pancreas, which was blocked. The procedure began at 4:30 p.m. When it was completed, the doctor informed me that he suspected cancer. I felt numb. *What does this mean for Ethan? What does this mean for me? The big C word! Where do we go from here?* Ethan did not become fully alert before I took him home at 7:30 p.m. The doctors tried to tell Ethan about his condition, but the sedative they administered caused forgetfulness. He couldn't wrap his mind around what they were telling him.

That night, I could not sleep. What would this mean for us? How would I tell Ethan such devastating news? It became my "privilege" to tell

Ethan when he awoke at 2:00 a.m. Ethan refused to believe me. His reasoning was, "They haven't proven it." How does one deal with a loved one who has cancer but refuses to believe it? I felt alone. We couldn't talk about it. What was he feeling? He refused to share his deepest feelings with me.

On February 5, 2005, Ethan developed pancreatitis and was hospitalized. All at once my life was turned upside down. I needed to contact the church in Yakima and let them know Ethan would not be returning that week. We had no idea how long this hospital stay might be.

Being retired military, we use the Madigan medical facility and hospital attached to Fort Lewis here in Washington. This facility is thirty-five miles south of our home. The drive includes I-5 through Tacoma. On a good day the trip can take forty-five minutes. During rush hour that same trip might take up to two hours or more. This became a daily trip for me. I was blessed, since most of my trips were against the commuting traffic.

We had no idea where this road of pain and suffering was taking us. I had a husband who did not want to talk about it. I felt cut off and alone.

MY WILL, GOD'S RESPONSE: GOD'S WILL, MY RESPONSE

My commitment to surrender my life and to follow Christ was being tested.

Are you facing difficulties in your life today? Is your faith being tested? Dare you surrender your life to God and allow him to take control?

Lord, you ask us to follow you. What does that mean? How do I even begin to follow you when the way seems so difficult? The Bible teaches us that you promise to be with us. Give us the strength we need for each day to follow you. Amen.

_____

_____

_____

_____

_____

_____

_____

_____

ALETHA **VOGES**

My Will: God's Response

Ethan began having one procedure after another to get his body chemistry back into proper function. This was taking a toll both on his body and on our spirits. My prayer for February 12 reflected my total dependence on God.

> Ask and it will be given to you; seek and you will find; knock and the door will be opened to you. For everyone who asks receives; he who seeks finds; and to him who knocks, the door will be opened.
>
> Matthew 7:7–8

"Lord God, heavenly Father, we come boldly knocking at your door, seeking your will, and asking for a miracle. We ask for a complete and miraculous healing of all that is preventing Ethan from eliminating the poisons from his body. May this healing be evident to

all the doctors that your name may be praised. This is our will.

"If that is not your will, heavenly Father, then we ask that you give each doctor, nurse, or technician the skills they need to do the very best job they can. Give the doctors wisdom to discover and successfully treat the problem."

Then I prayed, *"As our lives are touching those of so many others, may we reflect your love in our words and actions, and may they know they have also been touched by you."* I closed the prayer: *"We surrender our lives to your will that your name may be glorified. In Jesus' name, amen."*

Where are you headed in your life? Are you trying to do it your way? Is your will for your life in tune with God's will for your life? Is God using your pain to touch someone else?

_____

_____

_____

_____

_____

_____

_____

_____

_____

MY WILL, GOD'S RESPONSE: GOD'S WILL, MY RESPONSE

Pleading

As I was driving to Madigan Army Hospital for my daily visit with Ethan on Sunday, February 13, I was again pleading to God for a miraculous healing. I wanted to spare Ethan the long road ahead. While I was listening to an inspirational religious CD, I decided to check the traffic report as I drove through Tacoma. I hit the random play button instead. The first song to be played was "The Lord's Prayer." The phrase "Thy will be done" lingered in my consciousness. I felt God telling me that my will was not his will. So again I surrendered my will to God's will.

In the next song, the words "He walks with me and he talks with me and he tells me I am his own,"[1] filled my heart with hope. Through these words, God promised that although the road ahead would be rough, he would be with us every step of the way. (He kept this promise as we stepped forward and as we slid backward.)

The third song was "His Eye is on the Sparrow." "His eye is on the sparrow, and I know he watches me."[2] The reassurance that we were on God's radar and he was watching over us filled me with peace. I could trust his promises to be with us because he cares for every sparrow, and he certainly cares much more for us.

When I awoke the next morning, the words "showers of blessings and 10,000 beside" kept running through my mind. I sensed God telling me that although we would not have a miraculous healing, he was going to shower us with his blessings. As I look back over those long months, I see blessings in timing, in people, and in the depth of our spiritual growth.

Think back over your own life. Have you ever stormed heaven with your pleading for an answer to a problem? How did God answer your request? Can you see little blessings that God has given you amid trials and tribulations? Has his hand been on your life, protecting you from harm? Has he been carrying you through tough times? Give him thanks for these blessings of faithfulness.

Great is Thy faithfulness, Oh Lord my Savior,
Morning by morning new mercies I see,
All I have needed thy hand hath provided.
Great is thy faithfulness unto me.[3]

_____

_____

_____

_____

_____

_____

_____

_____

MY WILL, GOD'S RESPONSE: GOD'S WILL, MY RESPONSE

Comfort for Comfort

I worked as a tax preparer, and Ethan became sick at the busiest time of the season. With Ethan in the hospital, I would get up at five each morning and drive to Madigan Hospital, thirty-five miles away, to visit him. I would try to catch a doctor to see what the next step of Ethan's treatment would be. At noon, I would drive back the thirty-five miles to work, work from 1:00 to 9:00 p.m., go home for supper, look at e-mails and mail, and do the other everyday chores, then drop into bed around 11:00 or 12:00 p.m. The next day, I would begin the routine all over again.

This demanding schedule began to take a toll on me. I put my emotions on the shelf and proceeded on autopilot. Ethan, who had always been my strength, was becoming very weak. Now I felt that it was my turn to be strong. Where does one get the strength to go on during hard times? I found the only place where I could count on receiving strength was in clinging to the promises I found in the Bible. Many times I prayed, "God, your Word says…therefore I am holding on to this promise."

When Ethan had procedures, I would call work and tell them I would not be in. They then called my clients and rescheduled. Of course, when I did make it to work, the clients, as well as my co-workers, were eager to hear how Ethan was doing. There were many days when God brought clients to my desk who were hurting and in need of a listening ear or a word of comfort. Amidst my trials, God used me to share his love with hurting clients; some were encouraged to do difficult tasks because of my walk.

Has God used you to bring someone comfort while you were suffering? Maybe you have gone to cheer up someone in the hospital only to be blessed yourself by the visit. In their suffering they have brought you encouragement.

God never wastes our experiences. Leaning on Jesus, we grow stronger through trials. What we have learned by our struggles, he asks us to share with others walking with us.

Praise be to God…the Father of compassion and the God of all comfort, who comforts us in all our troubles, so that we can comfort those in any trouble with the comfort we ourselves have received from God.

2 Corinthians 1:3–4

When all my strength was gone and I was trying to keep my head above water, you, Lord, were faithful to never leave me. You gave me courage and strength. You kept me healthy. Thank you, Lord, for using me to bring hope and comfort to others during my time of questioning and struggle. May your holy name be praised for struggles you have turned into blessings. In Jesus' name, amen.

_____

_____

_____

_____

_____

_____

_____

MY WILL, GOD'S RESPONSE: GOD'S WILL, MY RESPONSE

From Peace and Tranquility to Crisis and Chaos

Life can change from peace and tranquility to crisis and chaos in an instant. Ethan had driven the 150 miles home from Yakima on Thursday, February 3, 2005. He had his first procedure (a stent placed at the head of the pancreas) on the fourth, was admitted to the hospital with pancreatitis on the fifth, had the blocked stent replaced on the seventh, had an external liver drain inserted on the ninth, had the stent removed on the tenth, had the liver drain replaced with a larger one on the eleventh, was diagnosed with an infection on the thirteenth, and had the blocked drain replaced again the afternoon of the fifteenth. Each procedure required some sort of sedative followed by a three-hour stay in the observation unit. The overall recovery times lengthened with each procedure.

Ethan had never been very sick throughout his life. This was a totally new experience for him. His job was to comfort others who were sick. He had sat at the bedside of many a veteran who suffered from cancer or some form of illness and had been their strength. With the sudden changes and challenges in his health, he became depressed. The doctors were concerned about how this depression was affecting his overall recovery.

The morning of February 16, the GI doctor told us that Ethan was not ready to go home. If he did go home, his condition would worsen. So I left Ethan visiting with our daughter Nan and went to work. No sooner than I got to work, I got a call from her saying they were discharging Ethan. Quickly completing the two clients waiting for me, I returned to the hospital. The internal medicine doctor thought going home would alleviate Ethan's depression. I did not know that the GI doctor had not been consulted. We were finally ready to leave the hospital at 5:00 p.m. Nan and I were both caught in the rush hour traffic as we returned to our respective homes.

Ethan was so weak that I called ahead to have some friends meet us to help get him into the house. After dinner, I could not get Ethan out of a chair and into bed. I went next door to get my strong neighbor to come and help. He brought his wife along. I found that she was studying to become a nurse. Several times she helped when I needed someone quickly.

Ethan and I only got half an hour to two hours of sleep at any one time. This lack of sleep on top of all the prior days of little sleep and constant travel left me totally exhausted. I had no strength of my own left. I could only go on because God answered the prayers for strength from all our friends.

Are you burdened by life's challenges? Do you feel totally exhausted? Christ comes to us in our weakness. We only need to acknowledge our weakness and ask for his strength. He is as close as a whispered prayer. Our situation may not change, but how we deal with that situation can.

Guide me O thou Great Redeemer,
Pilgrim through this barren land
I am weak but thou art mighty.
Hold me with thy powerful hand.
Bread of heaven, bread of heaven
Feed me now and evermore, feed me now and evermore.[4]

_____

_____

_____

_____

_____

_____

_____

_____

ALETHA **VOGES**

God Will Provide

Amidst our struggles and trials, God sends us his helpers. When Ethan was discharged, the orders said to come back for blood work, make an appointment with the releasing doctor, and to make another appointment with the GI doctor on February 22 or 23. When I called for the GI appointment, they wanted us to come in on the eighteenth instead. We didn't know at the time what a real blessing from God this would be.

By Friday morning, February 18, 2005, I was just going through the motions. Desperately in need of sleep, I called our church secretary to see if she knew anyone who could come over so I could get some sleep. I also told her about our trip to Madigan that day. She suggested I have someone go along with us to the appointments. I was too tired to argue. She contacted Kristi, who rearranged her schedule and accompanied us. Kristi, a recent widow of an oncology surgeon who had brain cancer, had been through all the struggles of losing a husband to cancer. She had walked the very path that I was now treading. The two of us became very close as the months passed. We had many long phone conversations when I just needed a friend.

Ethan had not eaten over 160 calories for breakfast and didn't want any lunch. Riding in a wheelchair, his first stop was the lab. The blood work draw went swiftly. We went to the sixth floor next to meet with the doctor of internal medicine. Ethan was becoming sicker by the minute, as Kristi could tell. After over an hour of waiting, she informed the doctor of Ethan's declining condition. He finally told us that Ethan was too sick; they would have to admit him for further evaluation if they were to be able to discover the problem. With that, they sent us to the GI clinic. Ethan was now refusing sips of water. Kristi's alertness to Ethan's declining condition prompted her to request a gurney for Ethan so he could lie down. The GI doctor took one look at Ethan, requested his vital signs be checked, and began IV fluids. I suspect he also called the lab to get an ASAP on the lab work. An hour later, he came in to tell us that Ethan's condition had worsened. His electrolytes were terribly out of balance, and he was in danger of renal failure. Ethan would need immediate hospitalization and was sent to the ICU.

Being totally exhausted myself, I felt now that Ethan was being admitted and the nurses would be caring for him, we could go home. Kristi asked, "Are you sure you want to go?"

I replied, "Yes. We won't be able to see him for a couple hours, and he probably wouldn't enjoy our company anyway."

The next day, Kristi asked me if I knew what the doctors were doing with Ethan. I said, "No." She told me they were performing life-support measures. I was too tired to realize the gravity of the situation.

The Whipple surgery Ethan needed so badly had to be postponed until the doctors could get his health back to some state of normalcy, and Ethan would be required to remain in the hospital.

At this point, I had a choice: I could choose to be bitter because of the internal medicine doctor's ineptness and spend my energy fighting the system. Or I could choose to look at the special people God placed in our lives to help us through this difficult time. I chose not to let bitterness sap my energy. Instead, I wrote a letter to the hospital explaining what happened and asked them to make sure nothing like that happened to anyone else. I was then free to use my energy to care for Ethan the best way I could. The hospital never denied any reasonable request I had from that point on.

Have you allowed a perceived injustice to sap your energy instead of letting go? Jesus endured the ultimate injustice when he died for us on the cross. Can we lay our injustices at the foot of the cross and move forward? God provided forgiveness for us in Jesus. He asks us to forgive those who have hurt us in any way.

Lord, when the days ahead are dark and foreboding, where can we go but to you? We cling to your promise to be with us every step of the way. While we are praying for miraculous healings of body, you are giving us, instead, peace of mind, strength for our emotions, and a contented spirit. For these and all the other blessings you are sending our way, we are thankful. Keep us always in your everlasting arms. Amen.

_____

_____

_____

_____

_____

_____

_____

_____

_____

MY WILL, GOD'S RESPONSE: GOD'S WILL, MY RESPONSE

Oh Lord, I Cry to You

This was my plea for February 19, 2005:

> Give ear to my words, O Lord, consider
> my sighing. Listen to my cry for help,
> my King and my God, for to you I pray.
> In the morning, Oh Lord, you hear my
> voice; in the morning I lay my requests
> before you and wait in expectation.
>
> Psalm 5:1–3

> The eyes of the Lord are on the righ-
> teous and his ears are attentive to their
> cry.
>
> Psalm 34:15

> Out of the depths I cry to you O Lord,
> Oh Lord, hear my voice. Let your ears be
> attentive to my cry for mercy.
>
> Psalm 130:1–2

What do you do when life throws you a curve? Where do you turn for strength? The psalmist found his strength in the Lord. We too can call on him to give us strength.

Lord, I cry to you for help. The road ahead seems like a long, dark tunnel. We seem to be taking baby steps, and it feels like it will take forever to reach the other side.

Fill us with your Spirit as we take this journey. Walk beside us and uphold us. Here in Seattle we speak of sun breaks. On rainy or cloudy days, the sun breaks through the fog or clouds to give us an emotional boost. So we ask you, Lord, to give us "sun breaks" as we travel this unknown path. May we feel the presence of your love all along the way until we reach the other side rejoicing.

We thank you for the many prayer warriors who are pleading our cause. We ask that you would bestow on each of them a blessing as we travel this road together. In Jesus' name, amen.

_____

_____

_____

_____

_____

_____

_____

_____

MY WILL, GOD'S RESPONSE: GOD'S WILL, MY RESPONSE

Jesus Only

When I left Ethan at the hospital on Friday evening, February 18, 2005, his life was in grave danger. But when I arrived Saturday morning, Ethan's condition had done a 180-degree turn. I said to him, "I'm sorry you had to take this detour in your healing."

Ethan replied, "No. This was not a detour. It is straight ahead. Nothing matters, not money, not job, not retirement, only Jesus." He began to face each day with a new strength from Jesus. All praise to God! Ethan wanted me to thank our family, our friends, those on our e-mail list and all the extended prayer warriors for their cards, e-mails, prayers, and acts of kindness toward us. He told me he felt the prayers and was overwhelmed by the outpouring of love shown to us.

In the afternoon as Ethan lay in his ICU bed, he was humming. I asked him what song he was thinking of. It was "Because He Lives," written by two of his favorite praise songwriters, Bill and Gloria Gaither.

> Because He lives, I can face tomorrow.
> Because He lives, all fear is gone.
> Because I know He holds the future,
> And life is worth the living, just because
> He lives.[5]

Have you had detours in your life? How has God used these detours? What blessings has God given you because of the new path you walk?

Because Jesus lives, we too can face whatever comes our way. His promises are new every morning, and in the evening he is with us as we rest in him. Thanks be to God for his unfathomable love to us.

Lord, so often our eyes are everywhere but on you. Forgive us for our unfaithfulness. Lead us to join with Ethan in saying, "Nothing matters, only Jesus." Amen.

_____

_____

_____

_____

_____

_____

_____

_____

MY WILL, GOD'S RESPONSE: GOD'S WILL, MY RESPONSE

E-mails

I knew early on I would not be able to keep every-one informed about what was happening. There were not enough hours in the day to personally talk to each family member. I began sending e-mails. Soon, others were asking to be placed on the list. The list grew to include over seventy names. Many people who received the e-mails were then forwarding them to other family and friends. Our son Nathan even sent them to friends and relatives in Germany.

I began hearing from people who the first thing they did in the morning was to check and see if there was an e-mail from me. I usually gave an update on our situation and closed with a prayer about our need for the day (like these devotion-als). Some nights when I tried to write an e-mail, it felt like a burden. I didn't feel like sharing my thoughts. Yet people wanted to hear from me. I would pray, and God would give me words. Then, exhausted, I would fall into bed.

I began hearing stories of how God was using our struggle to bless those who were reading the e-mails. One woman told me how her computer broke down, and she asked her husband, who didn't have time for God, to bring the e-mails home from work. He began reading the e-mails he printed. Soon he was attending church with her and wanted to join a Bible study. Another woman whose mother was in the last stages of life said rereading the e-mails gave her courage and hope. Yet another woman who was a preschool director began using the e-mails for staff devotions.

God was not granting Ethan the complete healing as I had pleaded. He was, however, answering the last part of my prayer: "As our lives are touching those of so many others, may we reflect your love in our words and actions, and may they know they have also been touched by you."

Has someone's actions brought you comfort? Whose life might you be touching today that needs to hear of God's love for them in Christ?

May these devotions be an extension of God's work in touching the lives of those who read them. May his name be glorified! Amen.

_____

_____

_____

_____

_____

_____

_____

_____

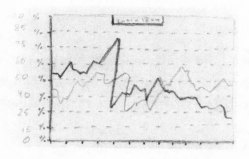

Roller Coaster Riding

Ethan would have a bad day. I would send out the e-mail sharing his condition. The next day might be a very good day. I would send out a glowing report, only to be followed the next day by another procedure or crisis. Our lives felt as if we were on a roller coaster ride that would not quit. We thanked God for all the good days. These were days of hope, thanksgiving, and praise. During the bad days, we clung to the promises of God's unfailing love for us.

God created our body chemistry to be very delicate. A slight imbalance can cause many problems. One of Ethan's reoccurring problems was a block in the liver drain that would cause his mental status to deteriorate. With his body chemistry balanced, he returned to his usual, chatty self. One day, Ethan asked me how I knew when he needed the liver drain changed. I told him that he was not himself and had trouble completing simple talks. This was one of the causes of the roller coaster rides. The drain was changed at least fifteen times during the fifteen months of procedures.

> For you created my inmost being; you
> knit me together in my mother's womb.
> I praise you because I am fearfully and
> wonderfully made; your works are won-
> derful, I know that full well. My frame
> was not hidden from you when I was
> made in the secret place. When I was
> woven together in the depths of the
> earth, your eyes saw my unformed body.
> All the days ordained for me were writ-
> ten in your book before one of them
> came to be.
>
> Psalm 139:13–14

Spend time thinking about how intricate your body is, how delicate the chemical balance. Only a loving God of creation can make and keep our bodies functioning properly. Where is God when our bodies are out of balance? Does he care if I hurt? The God who created us does care. He walks alongside us, giving us the strength to go on.

With the psalmist we praise your name, O Lord, for creating and sustaining our bodies. When our last hour comes, take these flawed bodies to live in perfect harmony with you. Amen.

_____

_____

_____

_____

_____

_____

_____

_____

MY WILL, GOD'S RESPONSE: GOD'S WILL, MY RESPONSE

Crisis

Before we were created, God had a plan for our lives. When trials come, and we know they will, he is as close as a whispered prayer. Sometimes it is hard to see what is happening in our lives. We want things to turn out as we have planned. God's way, however, may not be the same as our way.

The outcome was not what I had wanted or for which I had prayed. But through the entire ordeal, God's hand was upon our lives. For each crisis, God placed someone beside me to walk those difficult days with me. Sometimes it was one of our five children, other times it was my sister from North Carolina, or my brother and his wife from Iowa, and still other times dear friends from near and far. Having someone at my side gave me the strength I needed to go on while my world was falling apart.

MY WILL, GOD'S RESPONSE: GOD'S WILL, MY RESPONSE

My sister, Rhoda, is a nurse. Her valuable information and explanations of medical terms, doctor's lingo, body functions, and blood results proved to be invaluable to me as Ethan went from crisis to crisis. Although she lives in North Carolina, she was as close as my nearest phone. And she didn't mind calls at any time of the day or night.

With each crisis, God was preparing me for the final separation—Ethan's death. There, too, God's loving arms were around me to give me strength.

What type of crisis are you dealing with today? Are you trying to deal with it alone? Reach out to those people God has placed in your life to walk beside you and share his love. Reach out also to God, who gives us strength to go on amidst our crisis.

Lord, we do not know what tomorrow will bring. Will it be a day of love and joy? Will our tomorrow be filled with pain and strife? Will it be filled with death and separation? Whatever tomorrow brings, let me feel your love, and in that love, grant me strength to meet whatever comes my way through Jesus, my Savior and my friend. Amen.

_____

_____

_____

_____

_____

_____

_____

_____

MY WILL, GOD'S RESPONSE: GOD'S WILL, MY RESPONSE

God's Angels

While deadheading my daylilies one day, I contemplated why God would create a flower that would only bloom for one day. Here today and gone tomorrow. I then thought about the people who come into our lives for only one day. Why are they here? They are here today and gone tomorrow.

When Ethan was having a very low day emotionally, a "daylily" came to sit beside him and minister to him. This daylily was a nurse named Larry. Larry only worked that one night. He had time to sit and spend quality time with Ethan. Was this one of your angels, God?

How often do we miss God's special "daylilies" in our lives? Do we recognize the angels he sends? Think about your past. Has one of God's "daylilies" bloomed in your life?

"Do not forget to entertain strangers, for by so doing some people have entertained angels without knowing it" (Hebrews 13:2).

Lord, help me never be too busy that I miss the special people you place in my life, the daylily. Maybe you have placed me in the life of someone to be his or her daylily. Keep me in your will that I may be used by you. Amen.

Doctors, Doctors, Doctors

Ethan's condition had so many facets that he had several doctors. The GI doctor first suspected cancer. His favorite comment was, "It never presents itself this way." He was insisting on surgery as soon as Ethan's body could handle it. The surgeon wanted proof of what he was operating on before he proceeded. The internal medicine doctor was interested in Ethan's mental health in relationship to his healing. Then there were the interventional radiologists (IR) who kept changing the liver drains. Ethan developed MRSA, a highly contagious infection that can lead to death, and had an infectious disease physician. He was not eating properly and was assigned a nutritionist. His diabetes was watched by the endocrinologist. Who was watching over the whole picture? That job fell on my shoulders. Sometimes this responsibility felt overwhelming.

The doctors were talking about performing a "Whipple." This is a very delicate surgery in which they remove the head of the pancreas and the defective duct and reconnect it to the small intestine. There is a tiny drain in the pancreas that is the size of angel hair pasta that needs reattaching. God had provided a specialist for that procedure at Madigan. Dr. Martin, a national expert in the Whipple surgery, was a reservist here on active duty for nine weeks.

Dr. Martin told me his story. He was from Maine. An army hospital in Louisiana needed a surgeon. The first one assigned was a pediatric surgeon; however, they didn't need a pediatrician. A second surgeon from the Northwest was selected; he was unable to go either. Finally, Dr. Martin was selected. He should have been the last one contacted, as he had just been decommissioned from his tour in Iraq. They selected him anyway and sent him to Madigan before going to Louisiana. When he arrived, he was informed the slot in Louisiana had been filled. The army tried to send him to Alaska, but they didn't need a surgeon. The only other options were to keep him at Madigan, where he was excess, or to send him home. They kept him. God even used the United States Army to place the right surgeon here just to perform Ethan's surgery!

Are you keeping your spiritual eyes open to see how God is moving events in history for you? What "coincidences" have you had in your life? Were these really blessings from God?

We can only sit back in wonder and awe, O Lord, at your intervention in the history of our lives. May our minds always be attuned to the blessing you bestow upon us. Amen.

MY WILL, GOD'S RESPONSE: GOD'S WILL, MY RESPONSE

A Touch from Jesus

Ethan continued his slow progress to a somewhat improved health. Since he was hospitalized during Lent in 2005, the season took on a whole new meaning for me. The songs and messages brought insight deep within my soul.

My brother, Clifford, and his wife, Peggy, came to give me support. While we were at church, February 27, 2005, I was sitting in the pew praying and asking God if I should get our boys to come home before Ethan's surgery. As I was praying, I felt as if Jesus were giving me a hug. There seemed to be a presence over my right shoulder. My inner being felt that Ethan would be okay. I leaned over and told Peggy. She had just had a peace that Ethan would be all right. On the way to the car, the choir director stopped me and told me that during communion, she had a real sense that Ethan would be all right. Three messages with the same answer! I would not have to get the boys home now.

Brian had plans to come the first week in March when the surgery was scheduled. Nathan would come from Indiana for Easter, and Philip was coming home from California the following weekend. Little did I know just how God was orchestrating the timing of each visit.

How many times in life have we been so busy that we missed a special touch from Jesus? We feel we need to be always doing something. We live in an age of cell phones and iPods. We spend time talking on the phone or texting; we have constant music from the iPod; while at home the TV blares constantly; messages continually fill our mind.

How often do we take the time to allow God to speak to us?

God asks us to come away to a quiet place to clear our mind and to take some time to "Be still and know that I am God" (Psalm 46:10).

There we feel the love of Jesus and are strengthened.

May each of you feel the love of Jesus in your own life. May he strengthen you and give you peace as he did for us. Amen.

_____

_____

_____

_____

_____

_____

_____

_____

MY WILL, GOD'S RESPONSE: GOD'S WILL, MY RESPONSE

Preparing for Surgery

Brian had come from Las Vegas to be with me while Ethan was in surgery. It was scheduled for Monday, March 7, 2005. Since it would be an extensive surgery, they had the operating room reserved for the entire day. Our chaplain friend, Ted, had come to visit on Sunday to give Ethan communion. Later in the evening, Ethan was restless, and the doctors discovered that he was running a high fever, and his heart rate was drastically elevated. The doctor moved Ethan to the ICU where he could get more individualized nursing care. He had developed another infection.

Brian and I arrived Monday morning to learn that they had rescheduled the surgery for Wednesday morning. We went outside in the beautiful morning sun to make phone calls to the immediate family and then returned to Ethan's

ICU room. Upon arrival, the room was full, and we were told we could not go in. Ethan's heart rate had again skyrocketed, and his blood pressure had dropped dangerously low. They were ready with the shock paddles. The doctor informed us that they had discovered a yeast infection in the blood, and they could not operate until it was cleared. The surgery was rescheduled for the following week. We returned to our seats outside the hospital to call everyone back to tell them of the events and the change of plans. Brian had to return to Las Vegas, but, again, God had placed someone by my side while I had to deal with some tough days.

What tough days have you endured? Was there someone beside you to help carry your load? Maybe you have been the person who has supported someone else.

Lord, we are on your timetable. We like to think we have everything under our control. Yet when events over which we have no control invade our carefully planned schedule, we tend to become angry and lash out at you. What is your plan for our life? Why the delay? I only know that I must trust that you know best. Thy will be done. Give me patience to wait for your perfect timing. Amen.

ALETHA **VOGES**

_____

_____

_____

_____

_____

_____

_____

_____

_____

MY WILL, GOD'S RESPONSE: GOD'S WILL, MY RESPONSE

Peace

The world does not offer us any peace. What it does offer is stress over relationships, over financial issues, over safety, over retirement, and over health.

Ethan had been talking of doing an in-depth study of Job again. I told him he was living the life of Job, so now would be a good time to study it. Like Job, Ethan was living with seemingly daily crisis.

We question God's presence in our lives when everything around us seems to be falling apart. Where are you, God? Do you hear our cries? Where is that peace I read about in scripture? By God's grace, Job did not give up. I could do no less, and so I prayed that as Ethan awaited surgery, God would fill him with the peace beyond all understanding.

The only real peace comes from knowing Jesus Christ as our Lord and Savior and placing our faith and total dependence on him. Jesus is our all in all. He holds us up when we cannot stand on our own. Deep within our soul, Christ infuses us with a peace that we cannot understand, even though we are enduring trials and temptations. He rearranges events in history to do his bidding. Christ brought us healing when he died on the cross. It is to this faith we cling and in which we walk each day.

Are you crying out for peace in your life? Where are you looking for answers to your questions and cries for stability? God has a great exchange rate. He offers us peace and rest when we bring to him our struggles and chaos.

And so we come to you Lord and ask for your peace. We ask that our loving Father would pour upon us his peace that is beyond all understanding. We can do nothing to change the outcome of the events that are shaping our lives. However, we can still trust when it seems like there is nothing in which to trust. So we place our lives in the hands of the gentle Savior. May he grant us all the strength we need to accomplish great things for him. Amen.

_____

_____

_____

_____

_____

_____

_____

_____

_____

MY WILL, GOD'S RESPONSE: GOD'S WILL, MY RESPONSE

De-stressing

I had prayed for peace as my world crumbled. Sleep would not come. As I lay awake listening to the quiet music of the worship channel, words of Psalm 63 flashed on the screen.

O God, you are my God.
At dawn I search for you.

My soul thirsts for you.

My body longs for you in a dry, parched land where there is no water.

So I look for you in the holy place to see your power and your glory.

My lips will praise you because your mercy is better than life itself.

So I will thank you as long as I live.

I will lift up my hands to pray in your name.

You satisfy my soul with rich foods.

My mouth will sing your praise with
joyful lips.

As I lie on my bed, I remember you.

Through the long hours of the night, I
think about you.

You have been my help.

In the shadow of your wings, I sing
joyfully.

My soul clings to you.

Your right hand supports me.

Psalm 63:1–8, "God's Word" translation

I spent the next day trying to relieve the stress from my life. I became so relaxed that I fell asleep in the chair in Ethan's hospital room. He told me it was good to see me sleep.

Are you stressed and overwhelmed with life? Are you trying to handle everything on your own? God asks that we be honest with ourselves and with him. He lovingly waits for us to call upon him so he might show us his love and his power. Only when we lean on Christ can we find true peace.

Thank you, God, for removing the stress. Thank you for answering my prayer for peace. Amen.

_____

_____

_____

_____

_____

_____

_____

_____

_____

MY WILL, GOD'S RESPONSE: GOD'S WILL, MY RESPONSE

Surgery at Last

Ethan had four days with no crises, and the surgery proceeded on March 14, 2005. Rhoda and Nan were with me as we waited for what could be as long as eight hours. However, after only about one and a half hours, the doctor came to tell us the surgery was over since they were not able to do the surgery as they had planned. Ethan's gallbladder had many stones and was leaking, so he could only take it out. Dr. Martin told us that if he had proceeded, the surgery would not have been successful. With the pancreas still inflamed, we did not know if Ethan would need more surgery or not. He was doing very well for now.

And so we praise the Lord! What an awesome answer to prayer. God forgives all our sins of not trusting wholly on his will for our lives. It is so easy to doubt when everything goes against our plans. However, when we get down to grace and we can only look at Jesus, we really learn to trust on God for what is best for our lives. He heals our diseases. We felt as though we had come up from the pit to be showered with blessings.

Those who constantly held us up in prayer were a part of the blessings we received. They were our support when we were weak and exhausted. Their love and compassion for us brought us to tears. Now we waited for Ethan's strength to be renewed as the eagles. Our hearts burst with love, praise, thanksgiving, and peace.

How quick are we to trust God's plan for our lives? Do we criticize God for not giving us what we think is best for us? How do we know when God plans to turn our trials into blessings?

> Praise the Lord O my soul, all my
> inmost being praise his holy name.
>
> Praise the Lord O my soul and forget not
> all his benefits—
>
> who forgives all your sins and heals all
> your diseases,
>
> who redeems your life from the pit and
> crowns you with love and compassion,

who satisfies your desires with good
things so that your youth is renewed
like the eagles.

Psalm 103:1–5

Lord, our lives are in your hands. Open our eyes and help us see how you turn our struggles into blessings. Amen.

_____

_____

_____

_____

_____

_____

_____

_____

The Proverbial Planner

Ethan was a planner at heart. Late one evening in 1972, as I was frantically preparing for our young family to leave on vacation, Ethan was sitting at the table with the maps. I thought he was planning our trip until he said, "Next year, I think we should go..." I almost threw him out!

While in the ICU recovering from his surgery, he continued in his usual manner of planning. My sixty-fifth birthday was coming up, and he asked Rhoda, who was visiting, to be his personal shopper and get me a gift. He also plotted with his nurse Josie, who arranged for a slightly off-key septet of ICU nurses to sing "Happy Birthday." We dined on angel food cake and strawberries. After so many bad days, it was great to see Ethan engaging.

Ethan also liked to make sure everyone was having a good time. When visitors came, he felt

MY WILL, GOD'S RESPONSE: GOD'S WILL, MY RESPONSE

they should go out to see the town. He had suggestions for touristy activities, as well as restaurants they needed to visit. We dubbed him our "tour guide."

Amidst the days of struggle were days of sheer fun. Even though he was in ICU, he was engaging and full of mischief. Lord, we thank you for these wonderful memories.

Are your eyes open for those special moments? Do you take time to treasure each day? We can be so busy worrying about the difficulties in life that we miss the joy that is around us.

Lord, I thank you that we were able to have these joyful days interspersed with the struggle to live a normal life. Help me never to be bitter that I would miss the joy you send in my life. Keep me from becoming so busy that I do not have time to focus on all the blessings you have planned for me. Amen.

_____

_____

_____

_____

_____

_____

_____

_____

MY WILL, GOD'S RESPONSE: GOD'S WILL, MY RESPONSE

The Waiting

Now that the surgery was over, we were waiting for Ethan to get well enough to go home. The doctors tried to send him out of the ICU a couple times, but each time the receiving floor declined because of a medication they could not administer or a PICC line, for IV feeding, they could not monitor. Finally, on the afternoon of March 19, he was moved from the ICU to 7N, a regular ward.

The next step was to get Ethan strong enough to go home. Because of his history of roller-coaster ups and downs, they were not going to send him home before they felt it was safe. Would he need another operation to fix the pancreatic duct? Only time and waiting would tell.

How do we handle waiting? Are we patient? Can we sit back and wait for God's timing? Do we want life on our own time schedule? Are we ill at ease, so we lash out in anger? God reaches down to us when life becomes too much for us to handle. He infuses us with his power and love. Then we can go on, strengthened to meet each new challenge.

When we arrived at the hospital on March 20, Ethan said that the floor intern told him that his numbers looked good, and she thought he could go home the next day. I said, "Not!" He was still hooked up to numerous and sundry gadgets all over his body. I felt it would be good for him to try his wings as a non-bionic man for perhaps a day before I brought him home to life in the real world.

God is good! We must remember that we are on his timetable. We may want instant healing or gratification for our desires, but he knows what is best for us. We can only trust that we will have the patience to wait.

> We wait in hope for the Lord; he is our
> help and our shield.
>
> In him our hearts rejoice, for we trust in
> his holy name.
>
> May your unfailing love rest upon us, O
> Lord, even as we put our hope in you.
>
> Psalm 33:20–22

ALETHA VOGES

MY WILL, GOD'S RESPONSE: GOD'S WILL, MY RESPONSE

Nutrition

One of Ethan's trials was food. When he was first admitted, he was on water only for several days. Later, food did not taste good because of the metallic taste from all the antibiotics. Having been in the hospital for over six weeks, the menu became boring. He had tried everything and didn't like any of it anymore. I got permission to order from the cafeteria menu. I also began bringing in food from home and preparing it in the floor microwave. This helped somewhat.

We need food to fuel our cells for repair and energy. His lack of eating lengthened his stay in the hospital since he was not getting the nutrition needed for healing. Improvement came slower than the doctors had hoped.

We need spiritual food to fuel our spirit. To keep us whole and to repair the damage of sin, we need to feed on spiritual food. Daily Bible reading, corporate worship, prayer, and meditation all serve to fuel our sagging spirits.

How are you feeding your body? Your spirit?

Lord, bless us with healthy appetites to replenish our physical body and to refresh our spirits. In Jesus' name, amen.

_____

_____

_____

_____

_____

_____

_____

_____

Homecoming

Saturday, March 26, 2005, began as a day of apprehension and ended as a day of rejoicing. Both of us were a little concerned about Ethan coming home because of our last experience. Nathan's plan to come for Easter instead of for the surgery worked out perfectly. What a blessing! Having extra hands to help as I brought Ethan home was huge. We marveled at God's perfect timing.

Ethan went into the hospital the week of Ash Wednesday and came home on Holy Saturday. The Lenten season of 2005 had an impact on my heart as none other has. Every hymn, every Bible reading, and every sermon deeply touched my heart and soul. These struggles made the Easter service and Ethan's return home so joyous.

Christ is risen! He is risen indeed! My heart sang and rejoiced with tears of happiness just under the surface ready to burst forth.

Ethan shared with me that returning home turned the corner in his fight with depression. It gave him a new vision of what was yet before him. He told me he was convinced more than ever that God answers our prayers in his time for our benefit. Praise the Lord!

After being home for about five days, Ethan surprised me by climbing up the fourteen stairs to our bedroom. He had been practicing while I was at work. Ethan became determined to live a normal life.

What difficulties are you facing today? Where do you go for strength to help cope with these trials? Jesus is waiting for you to reach out to him in prayer and submission. When Christ Jesus died on the cross, he died for all the difficulties and trials we face. He died for our sins of trying to live life on our own. Oh, what joy it is to rest in his everlasting arms and be strengthened by his love!

Lord, as I face trials and tribulation, may I never forget your benefits for me. Help me to take my eyes off the trials of the day and instead help me to keep

my eyes focused on your love, which knows no bounds.
Praise your holy name! Amen.

_____

_____

_____

_____

_____

_____

_____

_____

MY WILL, GOD'S RESPONSE: GOD'S WILL, MY RESPONSE

Healing

Being home from the hospital did not mean we were free from doctors or appointments. We returned weekly to the Madigan Clinic for check-ups and procedures. The issue of the blockage at the head of the pancreas was still not addressed. With all their testing, they did not have a definite ruling on whether Ethan had cancer or not. The reports always said the cells were "suspicious." If the cancer was in the biliary lining, it might not show up on brushings they took. This would also be a very rare form of cancer. Dr. Martin, our Whipple specialist, had finished his tour and left Madigan, so we never found out if this was truly the case.

With Dr. Martin leaving, it meant we needed to get used to a new doctor. Since Ethan's case was rather unusual, most of the doctors had heard about his condition. They were having conferences as to what the next step in the process should be.

We continued to have the roller coaster ride with fevers, blocked drains, and emergency trips to the clinic for repairs. But the overall trend was going up. Praise the Lord!

Ethan became well enough for us to take our yearly after-tax-season trip to Las Vegas to visit with Brian and his family. As the granddaughters kept Ethan entertained, he unconsciously began to walk farther and to eat more. He regained much of the strength he had lost. Upon arrival home, he was able to see just how far the healing process had come. He walked farther with ease, and food tasted good again.

Are you impatient for God to send healing for your body? Are you waiting for a much-needed surgery? Lay your requests before God and ask him to give you peace as you wait for his perfect timing.

Lord, we know that you are in charge of the healing process. Sometimes we are too impatient. We know that your timing is perfect, but we ask for miracles anyway. Guide all doctors as they are used by you to affect the healing process. We rest in your almighty arms. Amen.

_____

_____

_____

_____

_____

_____

_____

_____

MY WILL, GOD'S RESPONSE: GOD'S WILL, MY RESPONSE

Decisions

Life began to become routine until Sunday, May 16, 2005. Ethan had been running a fever off and on for a few days. He was also not feeling well and agreed to go to the ER and get checked out. The doctors discovered further complications, including another infection. They admitted him to the hospital with the prospect of the Whipple surgery ASAP.

The vacation plans we had for the end of May were cancelled. Our future looked uncertain. We had been down this road before. We were totally at the mercy of our loving God and the doctors. We prayed for wisdom and skills for the doctors. We prayed for strengthening of Ethan's body to be in the best possible health, peace of mind for aid in healing, and a heart in tune with God's will for his life.

MY WILL, GOD'S RESPONSE: GOD'S WILL, MY RESPONSE

Our new doctor, Dr. Brown, wanted to do the surgery immediately. Ethan had built up confidence in Dr. Martin. Now he needed to put his faith in a totally unknown doctor. Doctor Brown had only performed thirty Whipples, while Dr. Martin had done over three hundred. Ethan told me that he felt like he was in a full-court press with his back to the wall. We were in favor of waiting a couple days to give the antibiotics a chance to clear out some of the infection. Dr. Brown agreed.

There are times in life when we need to make very difficult decisions. What do we use as our guide? How do we change our trust from one known to an unknown? When our backs are against the wall and the decision needs to be made now, how do we know we have made the correct decision?

For Ethan and me, it was back to prayer and our faithful prayer partners. We thanked God for the fifty days we had together. Feeling very inadequate to make this awesome decision, we prayed: *"Lord, you can see beyond today to the future. We ask that you give both Ethan and me the same message tonight as to what our next step should be. Give Ethan peace in the decision, confidence in the doctors, and a vision of how he can serve you after the surgery. Be with the doctors and grant them wisdom and steady hands to perform to the best of their ability. You, O Lord, can take us broken vessels and use us to your glory. You directed the United States Army to bring Dr. Martin here, and so now direct Dr. Brown and his team as you use them to accomplish your purpose. We surrender our lives to you, Lord. Use us to spread your love to the lives we touch. Amen."*

The next day, a dear chaplain friend, Bob, and his wife, Bobbie, visited Ethan. Chaplain Bob said that the moment he entered the room, his spirit was overflowing with peace, and it remained with him throughout the visit. Bob shared that at the April pastors' conference they had prayed daily for Ethan. On the final day, the floor was open for anyone to pray. Chaplain Bob prayed for wisdom and skill for the doctors during Ethan's surgery. People asked him if he knew something that the rest of them did not. Bob said he was just praying as he was led by the Spirit. In April, when no surgery was planned, Chaplain Bob was led to pray for the surgery. What an awesome revelation!

Ethan decided he could not survive without the surgery. He would put his trust in this new doctor to perform the surgery. With the decision to proceed with the surgery made, Dr. Brown scheduled it for Friday morning. Thursday became a day of preparation with exercising, resting, X-rays, and prayer.

What decisions are you forced to make today? Will these affect the rest of your life? Have you asked God to be a part of those decisions? Lay these requests at Jesus' feet and listen for his answers.

Lord, our lives are totally in your hands. We have prayed that our decision would be in your will. We pray that as we walk in that will, you will bless the outcome. Whatever the outcome, we know that you are with us through our difficulty and into each day in our future. To God be the glory! Amen.

_____

_____

_____

_____

_____

_____

_____

_____

ALETHA **VOGES**

Surgery II

Shortly after I arrived at the hospital at 6:45 a.m. on May 21, 2005, Ethan was taken to the operating holding room. Following our morning devotions, the head nurse joined us as I prayed for Ethan and the whole OR team. When Dr. Brown came by later, Ethan asked him if he could bless his hands. It was beautiful to hear Ethan praying for Dr. Brown and the whole surgical team.

Nan stayed with me the whole day. Our son Timothy spent the morning and evening with us. After eight and a half hours, the doctor came to tell us he was pleased with the overall surgery. They discovered cancer in the biliary duct, but they felt it was localized and no more treatment would be necessary. With the surgery complete, the focus turned to healing. We were advised Ethan would be in the hospital about two weeks following the surgery.

We thought Ethan would continue to improve. But this was not to be. We were still on the roller coaster, riding up one day and down the next. Each day had its challenges. We struggled through high fevers, low oxygen, low blood pressure, sitting up in the chair, no room in the step-down care ward, increased appetite, X-rays, CAT scans, blood draws, and dealing with edema from the surgery.

I prayed, *"My soul is weary, O Lord. Dare I ask for an afternoon without an issue? Dare I let my heart hope? Be with us, Lord, and give us strength for body, soul, and mind. We await the day we can come rejoicing. For now we can only say that you, Lord, are here, that you are in tomorrow, and that you are the God of healing. Thank you for healing; thank you for keeping me safe as I drive each day. Tonight we rest in your powerful arms. Amen."*

Are you facing issues in your life that seem to block your vision of God's answers to your prayers? Dare you hope for an end to your struggles? We only have today, so walk with God today. He will be waiting for you when you reach tomorrow.

_____

_____

_____

_____

_____

_____

_____

_____

_____

MY WILL, GOD'S RESPONSE: GOD'S WILL, MY RESPONSE

Where Can I Go but to the Lord?

The days following surgery were filled with a mixture of healing and continual challenges. There was sleeping and body recovery, spiking fevers, drastic oxygen drops, blood pressure in danger zones, plans to move to the next level of care, plans cancelled, X-rays, CAT scans, blood draws, and tests of all kinds.

> Find rest, O my soul, in God alone, my hope comes from him.
>
> He alone is my rock and my salvation; he is my fortress, I will not be shaken.
>
> My salvation and my honor depend on God; he is my mighty rock, my refuge.

Trust in him at all times, O people; pour out your hearts to him for God is our refuge.

Psalm 62:5–8

I arrived at the hospital on May 26, 2005, to find Ethan had again developed MRSA, a resistant staph infection. The CAT scan also showed a blockage in the left lobe of the liver; it was accidently sewn shut during surgery. *What else, Lord? Feeding tubes, liver drains, massive doses of antibiotics, insulin shots, and blood transfusions. When will this end?*

Where do we go when we are at the end of our strength? How much emotional roller-coastering can a body take? I can only join with the psalmist: "Why are you downcast, O my soul? Why so disturbed within me? Put your hope in God, for I will yet praise him, my Savior and my God" (Psalm 42:5).

No one has any answers. Where can we go but to the Lord? So, we put our hope in you, O Lord. Carry us when we are weary. Infuse us with your strength when ours is gone. Let us find peace and contentment in your almighty arms. Amen.

_____

_____

_____

_____

_____

_____

_____

_____

MY WILL, GOD'S RESPONSE: GOD'S WILL, MY RESPONSE

Rejoicing/Crying

What a glorious day Ethan had! I found him talking, smiling, planning, walking, and talking of being ready to write. What a dramatic turnaround from the previous days. The day before, he wanted to push the food under the bed. Now he was planning what he would like to eat. The doctors were talking of letting Ethan go home in the middle of the week. He was off all intravenous antibiotics and on to pills. I was taught how to care for all the drains and feeding tubes. At home, my friends helped me get the house ready with a bed downstairs. What a happy day!

When I arrived at the hospital the next day, June 8, 2005, Ethan told me he had endured a rough night. He couldn't keep anything down. By early afternoon, he asked me to get a doctor. They discovered his white blood count, which had been a respectable 9.6, was now a horrible 39. The doctor ordered more tests, and instead of going home, they sent him back to the ICU. This began a ride of more drains, good days, out of ICU, bad days, more drain changes, CAT scans, back to ICU, MRI, spinal tap, smiling, out of ICU, culminating with a twenty-one-day regimen of seven different antibiotics. Finally, Ethan began putting several days of improvement together.

Amidst life's challenges, all hope seems lost. We struggle to answer the question, "Why?" Where are you, God? Four times your word promises "you will never leave or forsake us" (Deuteronomy 31:6, Joshua 1:5, Psalm 94:14, and Hebrews 13:5). All we can do is trust.

Are you struggling to find answers in your life today? Are you asking, "Where are you, God?" Turn to the scripture passages above. Let the words sink deeply into your spirit, and trust God to answer in his timing.

Lord, we thank you that you hear each and every prayer we utter. Wrap your arms around us. Let us feel your presence. We pray for an end to our struggles. This is our will. We know your will is always best, even though it doesn't seem right at the time. And so we commend our lives into your hands. "Thy will be done." Amen.

_____

_____

_____

_____

_____

_____

_____

_____

MY WILL, GOD'S RESPONSE: GOD'S WILL, MY RESPONSE

Worry

I wrote these words on June 11, 2005: I awoke this morning to the strains of the chorus of "On Eagles' Wings" flowing through my head.

> And He will raise you up on eagles' wings,
>
> Bear you on the breath of God,
>
> Make you to shine like the sun,
>
> And hold you in the palm of His hand.[6]

I do not want to worry, and yet I think that is what I am doing. Of course, I tell myself that it is just concern, not worry. Lord, help me not to look at the unknown circumstances and conjecture what might come, but help me in my mind to focus on your love and grace. It is so very hard; yet you are all sufficient. The hymn writer of "Amazing Grace" said it well.

He will your shield and portion be

As long as life endures.[7]

A couple weeks ago you told me to surrender Ethan to you. I have been afraid of what that means. Are you gently telling me to prepare to live without him? Are you preparing me to hear bad news? Where does preparing for news that could be devastating begin and worry end? And God said, "Be still and know that I am God." Verse two of "It Is No Secret" brought me comfort.

There is no night, for in His light

You'll never walk alone.

Always feel at home wherever you may roam.

There is no power can conquer you, while God is on your side.

Just take him at His promise; Don't run away and hide.

It is no secret what God can do.

What He's done for others He'll do for you.

With arms wide open He'll pardon you.

It is no secret what God can do.[8]

What worries are sapping your energy or interrupting your sleep? Can you change the outcome of your situation by your worry? What can you do today that would eliminate your worries? Take the worries that you cannot change and lay them at Jesus' feet and leave them there.

Oh Lord, thank you that you care about all of our lives. Forgive us when we worry instead of trust in your love for us. Grant us your peace. Amen.

_____

_____

_____

_____

_____

_____

_____

_____

MY WILL, GOD'S RESPONSE: GOD'S WILL, MY RESPONSE

Blessings of Laughter

As we wrestled with the daily changes in Ethan's health, our support team gathered. Rhoda, Nathan, and dear friends Ruby and Ed descended upon us. Ethan, fresh out of the ICU, slid into his role as tour director, suggesting that we all go out and see the sights. On Sunday afternoon, as the tour director rested, the tourists could be found in the ward lounge asleep.

With three of our wedding attendants present, we planned to celebrate our forty-second wedding anniversary. Rhoda would leave the day before, so we celebrated on June 21, 2005, with balloons and gifts. I had been having increasing reoccurrences of chest pains, and while taking Rhoda to the airport, she made me promise to get checked out. On our anniversary, I had another episode and decided to go to the ER. They kept me all day and overnight. While I was stuck in the ER holding area, Ethan, Nathan, Ruby, and Ed were sharing jokes, puns, and having a jolly good time. (An episode a few days later led me to discover I was having reactions from my cholesterol medication.)

The doctors talked about how the antibiotics were helping Ethan heal. I feel that the fun and frivolity of our visit with Ruby and Ed contributed greatly to Ethan's overall mental and emotional healing.

Are we having enough laughter in our lives? With the stress of everyday living, we become so caught up in accomplishing "stuff" that we miss out on the sheer fun of laughing. How can you add laughter to your life?

Lord, you created us with a sense of joy and laughter. May we always remember to keep good, clean fun and laughter as a part of our daily lives. Amen.

_____

_____

_____

_____

_____

_____

_____

_____

_____

MY WILL, GOD'S RESPONSE: GOD'S WILL, MY RESPONSE

Death Amidst Life

While Ethan slowly became stronger, his sister Joanie became weaker from her battle with cancer that began in her lungs and ended in her liver and pancreas. She died on July 1, 2005. We thought back to the quick trip we had made to Portland to visit her just two days before this long hospital stay began. We thank God for this blessed opportunity to visit her during what was a difficult road for both Ethan and Joanie.

The doctors talked of releasing Ethan on July 6, the day of Joanie's committal. I asked if Ethan could stay one more day so Nan and I could represent the family at Joanie's service. Timothy and his family were also able to attend. The doctors agreed that one more day would give the social worker time to iron out some of the difficulties she was having about who would pay for the nursing care she had arranged for Ethan at home.

What are you doing today that will ensure you have no regrets when a loved one dies? Are there unresolved issues that need discussion? Do you need to forgive or ask for forgiveness of anyone? Have you just let time and distance create a wedge in your relationship?

Lord, our days are numbered. Help us always to be quick to forgive, quick to ask for forgiveness. May we not lose touch with our family or our friends, but hold them in our hearts and lives. Today might be the last chance we have to make a connection or heal a hurt. Help us to treat others as we want to be treated, with our time, our love, and our respect. Bless our relationships, Lord. Amen.

_____

_____

_____

_____

_____

_____

Healing and Home

As Ethan began feeling better, we received off-floor privileges. I was able to take him by wheelchair outside to enjoy the sunshine and watch the swans chase the geese families from the hospital pond. We also shopped in the hospital post exchange (PX) and bought a latte. After fifty days of hospitalization, the ride in the sunshine cheered Ethan's spirit.

Timothy's nine-year-old son came to visit Grandpa and played some songs on his recorder. Not only did Ethan enjoy this impromptu concert, but the other patients on the ward and the nurses did as well.

Philip and Christina, our youngest son and his girlfriend, came from California to spend the Fourth of July with us. They bought a king crab leg at Pike Place Market in Seattle and prepared it for

Ethan. What a treat from the usual hospital menu, which never changed.

When Ethan was fortunate, his room faced east. Beautiful sunrises and sunsets over Mount Rainier greeted him each day. And all day long, the ever-changing cloud formations revealed the beauty of God's creation. God's beauty brought healing to Ethan's spirit while cancer took its toll on his body.

After all the roller coaster rides Ethan had gone through, he still climbed eighteen steps during his physical therapy evaluation. Ethan had finished his twenty-one-day regimen of seven different antibiotics, and his day nurse rewarded him with a Baby Ruth candy bar.

Fifty-three days after his re-admittance, Ethan was released on July 7, 2005. Hallelujah!

Looking for joys changes our perception of the events ruling our lives. We can choose to dwell on each and every problem we face and become overwhelmed by life. However, instead of being overwhelmed by life, we can focus on God's activity in our lives and be filled with joy.

Where is your focus? Is it on the problems you face, or is your focus on how God is using these problems to draw you into a closer relationship with him?

Lord, we praise and thank you for all the blessings. Let us not continually look at the problems but lift our eyes to you and your glory. Amen

_____

MY WILL, GOD'S RESPONSE: GOD'S WILL, MY RESPONSE

Cancer

Ethan shared these words on cancer.

"The big *C* word is not the only word we need to keep in mind when we talk about healing. Other *C* words are compassion, care, commitment, and Christ. The doctor has said maybe as far as cancer is concerned. We always pray for healing when it comes to cancer. People have been known to live with cancer in remission. People have also lived a very short time. In this balance of life, we face each day by the grace of God. Be it one hour or ten years.

"Living by faith requires trusting in God's plan for our lives. Dying can be a beautiful thing. My prayer is when that last hour comes that I would be in the company of family to share with them the gate to glory. Everything is in the hands of God."

MY WILL, GOD'S RESPONSE: GOD'S WILL, MY RESPONSE

Has your life been touched by the big *C* word? With that one word, our world can be turned upside down. Fear and questioning control our thinking. How bad is it? Will I survive? How will my loved ones get along without me? Who controls our future? Praise be to God that he is right beside us, waiting for us to call on him in faith.

Lord, we fear the C word. Sometimes we feel almost paralyzed. We forget that you are there beside us. You are not a God of fear, but of hope and a future. We do not know the future, but you do. We place our lives in your control. Infuse our spirits with the power of your Holy Spirit that we may rest in you. Amen.

Vacation

I had reservations for the two of us to attend the LWML Retreat at Gig Harbor, Washington, from September 30 to October 2, 2005. Since the setting was in a hotel, I felt Ethan would enjoy the change of scenery and could rest there as well as at home. Life would not be so easy, however. Ethan became jaundiced on September 28, so we were back at the hospital for drain changes. They kept him overnight for observation. When I picked him up on the thirtieth, I took him directly from the hospital to the hotel. The hotel was about twenty minutes from the hospital, ten of which were on our way home anyway. Our room was on the first floor just a short distance from the meeting room. There, in a setting where Ethan was familiar to many, one hundred women fussed over him.

Ethan wanted to take a vacation from all the doctors and just get away. The doctors encouraged us to travel as long as Ethan felt up to it. He had finished his tube feedings, so with fear and trepidation mixed with desire and hope, I scheduled the trip from October 18 to 27, 2005. I purchased tickets on Southwest Airlines for a flight to North Carolina to visit Rhoda and John. Because our future always looked iffy, I always booked with Southwest. With them, I would not lose any money and could reschedule any time within a year using the same funds.

Life continued to be a challenge. Ethan was back for drain changes on October 3 and again on the twelfth. Our trip plans began to look doubtful. Pastor Gene and his wife, Joyce, stopped by on October 4. While he prayed for our trip, I felt excitement that our trip was a real possibility. If I looked at the circumstances, it looked bleak. If I looked to what God can accomplish, the sky is the limit. We live by faith, not by sight.

On the seventeenth, Ethan was feeling well enough, so off we flew to North Carolina. The change of scenery was great, as well as the mental stimulation of traveling and visiting. On Friday, we drove to Durham to see the sights. Ethan even walked across the front yard and up the steps of the Duke University chapel in Durham, North Carolina.

At about midnight, Ethan became very confused. As he stood to walk, he was unable to process which foot to move without my gently touching the back of each heal. We were able to get him back to Durham to the VA Hospital ER. The doctors asked questions to see how he was processing information. Through a series of questions, they would determine if Ethan's ammonia levels were causing mental confusion. One of their favorite questions was, "Who is the president?" Ethan's usual answer was, "Gerald Ford." After checking him over and giving us some medication, they sent him home. Saturday morning, Ethan was worse. With the help of the local EMTs, we got him into the car and went back to the VA Hospital. When he was questioned by the doctors this time, he could not give them his name, so they admitted him.

At the time we left Ethan at the hospital that evening, he still did not know who he was or where he was. His hands were bound in white gloves so he wouldn't pull out his tubes. When he awoke in the morning, the medication had cleared his thinking. Seeing his bound hands created fear in his heart. He realized that he had no idea where he was or where I was. Ethan told me later that he thought I had left him. This broke my heart.

I quickly got a crash course in balancing protein needed for blood vessel health while avoiding the high ammonia levels of too much protein, which caused mental confusion and impaired mobility. When Ethan's ammonia levels rose slightly, these functions plummeted like a rock. The medication Ethan took aided in ridding the body of the ammonia. By Sunday afternoon, the doctor discharged Ethan, armed with a refill of the medication, off we went. The tour director was ready to tour and enjoy the rest of the vacation. Just like that, with body chemistry in balance, Ethan became his cheerful, ready-to-go self.

How quick are we to get past the downturns in our lives? Do we hang on to the hurts and disappointments, or do we let go and look for brighter days ahead? Some days "we can't see the forest for the trees." We become so busy trying to control each minute detail of our lives that we miss the big picture. I found happiness when I let go and let God take control.

Lord, let me not be so focused on the trials and tribulations of this life that I neglect to focus on the blessings you give me. Thank you for each new day to serve you. Amen

_____

_____

_____

_____

_____

_____

_____

_____

Patterns

We walk day by day, step by step. Each step we take is directed by God. These steps form a pattern of our life, a patchwork quilt, if you will. Today we see the mangled threads on the underside and are oblivious to the beautiful pattern being created on top. One day we will see the whole pattern that made up our life.

We arrived home safely on October 27, 2005, but Ethan soon began feeling poorly. So, we went back to Madigan Clinic where the interventional radiologist (IR) replaced the liver drain again. Ethan would spend three hours in recuperation before I could take him home. While he recuperated, I shopped for groceries. At the commissary, a woman came up to me and said, "I know you." She worked in the ICU and had cared for Ethan. The nurse spent ten minutes explaining to me in language I could understand how the kidneys and liver process ammonia and how lactulose processes it. What an unexpected blessing from God! So much of the time, I didn't know what information I needed to know and had no clue what questions to ask the doctors.

Ethan continued to sleep most days and became lethargic. We took another trip to the IR doctors. The drain was not plugged. What could be the problem? Dr. Brown stopped by the recovery room to talk with Ethan. Because of Ethan's lethargy, Dr. Brown decided Ethan should spend the night in the hospital for observation and to allow them to perform more tests. Everything checked out okay except his liver numbers. We decided to take Ethan off all but the extremely necessary medication to take the strain off the liver; then I could add back medications as I saw the need. By that time, I was becoming so knowledgeable that people thought I was an RN.

My ever-loving, roller-coaster husband! I began to see a pattern. The highs trended lower, and the lows sunk lower as well. It is hard to watch your loved one continually become weaker, especially when the caretaking depends on what you do or do not do and what problems you catch and which ones you miss. As I struggled to find my way, I relied on the words from Saint Paul when he was tested. God's words to Paul were, "My grace is sufficient for you. My power is made perfect in weakness" (2 Corinthians 12:9).

Are there areas of your life that need an infusion of God's power? Have you confessed your inadequacies and asked for his power? I found that God was just waiting for me to acknowledge my weakness so he could give me his power.

I prayed, *"God, in my weakness fill me with your power. Amen."*

_____

_____

_____

_____

_____

_____

_____

_____

MY WILL, GOD'S RESPONSE: GOD'S WILL, MY RESPONSE

Thanksgiving

The reduction of medications brought some improvement. Philip asked us to spend Thanksgiving with him and Christina and her family in Pasadena, California. He planned to ask Christina to marry him and wanted us to be there to meet her family. Ethan's health improved enough for us to make the trip. We flew to Ontario, California, on Wednesday, November 23, 2005, and then drove to Pasadena. Ethan and I enjoyed four wonderful days of visiting and touring. It was great to see Ethan engaging and having a good time.

Philip and Christina flew back to San Francisco while Ethan and I had another day in the California sun. On Monday, November 28, we drove to Yorba Linda, California, and toured the Nixon Library. Ethan began to be cold. At the motel that night, I took his temperature. He was running a high fever.

MY WILL, GOD'S RESPONSE: GOD'S WILL, MY RESPONSE

I was scared to death. What could I do? We were in an unknown area, not close to any restaurants or stores, in a motel with only a limited menu, and I didn't want to leave Ethan for long. I hadn't packed any aspirin and had only one Tylenol PM. I did what I could to get the fever down and prayed a lot. I called my prayer partners back home to get some added prayers going on Ethan's behalf. Then I went to the bar and purchased a little food and took it to the room. Needless to say, I didn't sleep much that night.

Tuesday, we left to fly home. Ethan continued to run a fever, but not as high. Our plane was delayed leaving southern California and again in Oakland. Would he be able to endure the delays and get home safely? I just kept praying that he would. We were originally due to arrive home around 3:00 p.m. but didn't get in until almost 8:00 p.m. We spent the entire next day at Madigan Clinic getting Ethan's medications adjusted. I was so stressed that I do not remember which doctors we saw or what they did.

What a blessing that Christina's family had the opportunity to meet and get to know Ethan. Ethan enjoyed most of the trip.

These and all other gifts from God give us cause to offer our thanks. We thank God for doctors and nurses who lovingly cared for Ethan. We thank God for friends and family who seemed to show up just when we needed help. We thank God that I remained healthy and able to care for Ethan. We thank God that we had fifteen months to learn how to depend totally on him. I thank God that when Ethan's last hour came, he slipped quietly from this world to eternal life in heaven. Praise be to God!

For what are you thankful?

_____

_____

_____

_____

_____

_____

_____

_____

MY WILL, GOD'S RESPONSE: GOD'S WILL, MY RESPONSE

The Christmas Holidays

Mid-December Ethan was readmitted to the hospital. After three days of testing and new medications, they released him. Before I could take Ethan home, he insisted he needed to go to the PX to do his Christmas shopping. Armed with a scooter, he took off around the store. It never ceased to amaze me how a man so sick one day could force himself to do so much the next.

Philip and Christina came from California to enjoy the days with us. We drove an hour to Olalla, Washington, and spent Christmas Day with Nan and her family. Timothy and his family also stopped by. Nathan came for a visit in January.

The days were good until December 28, when Ethan's ammonia levels rose again. I caught it before it was so high that he needed to stay in the hospital. I could care for him at home. I had

MY WILL, GOD'S RESPONSE: GOD'S WILL, MY RESPONSE

to make a decision. Either I put Ethan in a home and have someone else care for him so I could work, or I could retire and care for him myself. We didn't need my income to pay bills; it was just fun money. I didn't think twice. So, after twenty-three years as a tax preparer, I retired.

New Year's Day was a time to reflect on the year past and look forward to where God was leading us. We live in an unsettled world with wars, catastrophic weather patterns, diseases of all kinds, and financial challenges. Looking back, we lived through many difficult days. These days also brought blessings without measure.

How does one evaluate the past year? Did I accomplish everything I set out to do? Did God have other plans? Am I looking at these alternate plans as a detour, or am I looking at them as where I am really supposed to be? How can I take the lessons from the past year and really learn from them? How will I change my expectations for the coming year? I can only rest in God and try to follow his leading in my life.

Lord, let me choose each day to be on the path you have chosen for me. Amen.

_____

_____

_____

_____

_____

_____

_____

_____

MY WILL, GOD'S RESPONSE: GOD'S WILL, MY RESPONSE

Questions without Answers

At our weekly appointment with the surgeon on February 1, 2006, Dr. Brown told us that Ethan would not live a long life. The roller coaster rides were trending downward. I longed to know how Ethan felt. But he was not sharing his deepest feelings. How long is "not a long life"? I had been through so many ups and downs that I was numb. I couldn't scream; I couldn't cry. I felt as if my emotions were sitting up on a shelf. Following my stubborn German upbringing, I continued to put one foot in front of another and plod on. My total focus was on doing what was best for Ethan to make him comfortable.

Ethan would not talk about his illness. I felt left out. He waged his battle with death in his own quiet way. It made me angry at first, until I decided that this was how he was choosing to deal with the cancer, and I had to honor his decision.

Five days later, on Monday, February 6, 2006, Ethan's drain and incision were oozing, and his mental status began declining again, indicating high ammonia levels and a need for a liver drain change. Back to Madigan. Since Ethan did not have an appointment, we waited until the doctors had an opening when they could do the procedure. I felt things were serious when both of the IR doctors took us into the conference room to discuss our options. They wanted to insert a permanent drain. I asked Ethan, as I always did, "Can I ask the hard question?"

He agreed, so I asked the doctors how long the permanent drain would last. They said it would probably be good for six to nine months. Ethan told them he wanted the external drain that could be changed. When Ethan was getting prepared for the procedure, I asked the IR doctor how much time he thought Ethan had left. He told me Ethan had about three to six months to live. I never told Ethan about our conversation. My world was falling apart before my eyes. In just five days, Ethan's short life had become three to six months. I called to talk with all the children and told them they may want to plan to make a trip to Seattle in the next couple months if they wanted to spend time with their father once more.

The IR procedure didn't begin until late in the afternoon. I knew that with Ethan's mental status declining and having just had the procedure, I would not be able to care for Ethan at home that night. I requested that he be able to stay at the hospital overnight, so the doctors agreed to keep him for observation.

On Tuesday, February 7, Ethan continued to be lethargic as an unknown infection and blood clots became a concern, especially a clot in the portal vein that feeds the liver. The internal medicine doctor felt Ethan had only days to weeks to live and said that I should take him home for care and comfort. What happened to our three to six months? Now I was told to take him home to die. I called the boys and told them to make reservations and come home immediately if they wanted to see their father one more time. I would pay for the plane tickets. I didn't want money to be a stumbling block in whether they could come home or not. Ethan was a very sick man.

Where are you, God, when I need answers? Where are you, God, when fear seeps into my every thought?

MY WILL, GOD'S RESPONSE: GOD'S WILL, MY RESPONSE

Is it because I have taken my eyes off of you? Help me to refocus and trust that you know what is best.

Are you facing questions without answers? Does God seem silent? Take all your cares and questions to the Lord in prayer and wait for his answers.

Lord, we come to you not knowing how to pray. I know you are a God of miracles. Do I hope for a miracle? What is your will for our lives? Your Word tells us not to doubt. I do not doubt that you can perform a miracle. But is that the best answer for us? Today, I have only questions. I have no answers. I just ask that you be with us each and every minute of each and every day. Give me the wisdom to make the correct decisions. I must rest in knowing that you, O Lord, know what is best for us and will accomplish that in our lives. In Jesus' name I pray, amen.

_____

_____

_____

_____

_____

_____

ALETHA **VOGES**

Sadness to Blessing

On Wednesday afternoon, February 8, 2006, Dr. Brown came by and asked what we were doing in the hospital. I informed him of the past three days' events. There was a ray of hope as Dr. Brown took over Ethan's care and began giving rapid-fire instructions to his intern.

Ethan slept all day Thursday. He refused food and drink. Dr. Brown told me that if the medications did not take effect, he would give Ethan twelve to twenty-four hours to live. If Ethan's numbers plummeted during the night, he would meet us there at the hospital. Things looked bleak.

After 6:00 p.m., Ethan woke up and asked for food. With the cafeteria closed, we fed him what we could find in the ward refrigerator. I went home feeling much better than I had felt all week.

MY WILL, GOD'S RESPONSE: GOD'S WILL, MY RESPONSE

Friday morning, February 10, Nan and I found Ethan sitting up, buttering his pancakes. His cheerful self was back. I told him he had given us quite a scare. He said, "I did?" I told him what had happened and how I had called the boys home. He also asked to see our granddaughters from Las Vegas. A quick phone call to Brian's wife, Pam, and she was making reservations for herself and the girls. By nightfall, Ethan was making puns with Nathan, who had arrived.

On Sunday, February 12, I took Ethan from the hospital to Timothy's home where our entire family spent two and a half hours together. Because our family lives scattered across the nation, we had not all been together in thirteen years. What a blessed time we had!

When Ethan became tired, I took him home. Timothy and his family stayed at home, Nannette and her family returned to Olalla, while Brian, Pam and the girls came to the house, as did Philip and Christina, and Nathan. With everyone gathered around Ethan's bed, he told them how proud he was of each of the children and what they had accomplished with their lives. He told them of his love for them. He never returned to that reflective state of mind again.

Had Ethan not taken this drastic downturn in his condition, we would never have had that special time together. Again, God was orchestrating events to give us a blessing. Praise his holy name!

Has a tragic event in your life turned into a blessing? What blessing might you have missed if you had taken a different path in your life?

Thank you, Lord, for allowing us to have these precious hours where we could be a support for one another. Whatever lies ahead for us, we will always remember the love and support from our family time together. Amen.

_____

_____

_____

_____

_____

_____

_____

_____

MY WILL, GOD'S RESPONSE: GOD'S WILL, MY RESPONSE

Record Keeping

When Ethan became ill in February 2005, it became necessary for me to take detailed notes and instructions. The first night he came home, we had missed a couple tasks. The doctors also liked to ask multiple questions, wanting information that I would not remember. I made computer printouts for everything. Each day, Ethan would take a multitude of medications at different times, sometimes hourly. I created a daily log to help us remember when to give medications, to keep blood sugar results, and to record other important data. Some records I kept in graph form so we could see trends. My record keeping became vitally important.

In March of 2006, I had another chest pain episode. *What do we do?* Ethan was at home, and I couldn't leave him alone. Who could I get to stay with him and still have someone to drive me? Dear friends from church, Leon, Jackie, Dennis, and Kristi, came to our rescue until Nan arrived to stay with her dad. They got safely through the day using Ethan's directions and my meticulous list of what needed to be done and when. The doctors decided to keep me in the hospital overnight. Nothing significant was found.

Sometimes my compulsiveness gets me into trouble. This time, it proved to be invaluable.

What is your dominant personality trait? How has God used this trait to bless you or someone else?

Lord, it never ceases to amaze me how you use each of our idiosyncrasies for some good. You have created us to be the people we are. May we always look for ways to use all the gifts you give us in ministry for others. Thank you, Lord, for loving all of me. Thank you for all the ways you use each part of me to your glory. Amen.

_____

_____

_____

_____

_____

_____

_____

_____

_____

MY WILL, GOD'S RESPONSE: GOD'S WILL, MY RESPONSE

Ethan's Last Days

Ethan's sixty-seventh birthday was approaching on April 23, so I sent out a request for cards from my e-mail contacts. He received over one hundred cards. People shared with him the blessings they had received from his ministry to them. Their messages blessed Ethan immensely.

Philip planned to spend a week at home with us starting on April 29, 2006. On Easter Sunday, April 16, Ethan became very weak. He was retaining fluid in his legs, was in need of oxygen, had begun turning yellow, became mentally confused, and did not eat. Ethan was on hospice care but really wanted to be able to see Philip one more time. I took him off hospice briefly while he was hospitalized to correct the dehydration and ammonia issues. It was a very difficult week. While he was mentally alert, his body began to shut down.

MY WILL, GOD'S RESPONSE: GOD'S WILL, MY RESPONSE

I was told that I should do what I could to make his last days comfortable. Brian came for Ethan's birthday, and on April 22, he helped me bring Ethan home.

During that last week of Ethan's life, the tasks became too much for me. I hired twenty-four-hour assistance and kept Ethan at home. Each helper would stay two or three days. We had a baby monitor in the bedroom of the person responsible for getting up when Ethan needed help. I took the monitor every other night so I could keep up with his nightly needs. Having brought Ethan home for his last days, I wondered how I would feel about having him die at home. Our friend Kristi said, "Why, your home will be the gateway to heaven!"

Ethan was on IV fluids to help keep his ammonia levels in check, but the extra fluids were creating a problem with edema. The night of April 29, Ethan was in great pain because of the edema. His body could not remove the fluids fast enough. I asked him if he thought we should forgo the IV fluids for the night and restart them in the morning. He agreed. At this point, I was withholding life support. My mind went back to September 2003, when in a skit at the LWML retreat, I played a woman who had to make life support decisions for her hospitalized husband. Little did I know that God was preparing me to make that very difficult decision myself by practicing it in a skit.

Philip and Christina arrived about 9:30 p.m. on April 29. It soon became evident Ethan wouldn't last through the night. We took turns being with him. The physical and emotional strains were taking their toll on me. At about 2:00 a.m., I was exhausted, but I just had to stay awake and be with Ethan. Philip put a chair beside the bed. With my head on a pillow next to Ethan's pillow and my hand on his chest, Ethan went to be with Jesus at 4:50 a.m. A beautiful smile on his face spoke volumes.

He was gone, and we were numb. Philip and I cried together and hugged each other. We made all the necessary phone calls. The girl from the agency was extremely helpful. She knew what I needed to do. Since Ethan was on hospice care, they would not need to do an autopsy, and we called the mortuary. They did not come to get Ethan until about 8:30 a.m. We continued to walk around in a daze and shared hugs. Nan arrived just as they were taking Ethan away. She took over

MY WILL, GOD'S RESPONSE: GOD'S WILL, MY RESPONSE

in helping make all the necessary plans and decisions. I could let go.

Do you know Jesus Christ as your Lord and Savior? Are you ready to die today? We do not know when our last hour will be. Jesus' death on the cross to pay for the sins of all mankind assures me I too will inherit eternal life in heaven with Jesus at his forever party. There, I will see Ethan again.

Lord, we make plans with no thought of you or your plan for our tomorrows. Yet we are nothing without you. Forgive our selfishness and wash us with the blood of Jesus. Make us fit to inherit eternal life. May we always be ready to hear you call our name. Amen.

_____

_____

_____

_____

_____

_____

_____

Be My Valentine

Ethan was in the hospital over Valentine's Day in 2005, so a dear chaplain friend, John, volunteered to play cupid for him. When I arrived home from work, John pulled up behind me. That was truly God's timing since I never knew when I would arrive home. John had seven red heart balloons and a dozen red roses, one balloon for each of our seven grandchildren.

A year later in 2006, Ethan was released from the hospital just before Valentine's Day. And again Chaplain John showed up at my door, this time with five red heart balloons and a dozen red roses, one balloon for each of our five children.

Chaplain John stopped by for a visit on April 21, 2006. Ethan insisted that I go to the store and purchase a latte so he could share it with John.

Just nine days later on April 30, Ethan would leave this earth to spend eternity in heaven.

I was missing Ethan, my Valentine, in 2007. When I looked out at the deck on February 15, I noticed two red heart balloons tied to the railing. I cried, but I knew just who my angel was: Chaplain John. He had stopped by the evening before and placed them there where I would find them. What a blessing Chaplain John has been in our lives.

Has God placed a special someone in your life that knows just what you need and has perfect timing? Give thanks to God for them.

Lord, we thank you for the many ways people touch our lives. When trials come, we can be so discouraged that we forget to see you in the people that you place in our lives. Give us also the vision to help others in your name. Amen.

_____

_____

_____

_____

_____

_____

_____

Grieving

What does grieving look like? How do you grieve the loss of someone with whom you have lived almost forty-three years? When does grieving begin? These were questions I grappled with over the months. As I look back, I can see that my grieving began long before Ethan died. Each time I cried out to God in prayer, I was grieving. Each time I heard his answer, I was healed in a small way. Today, my heart is at peace.

Each of us will grieve in a different way. We grieve differently for each person to whom we must say good-bye. How does it look? No one can answer that but you. I do know that grieving with the knowledge that we will meet together in heaven one day filled me with hope and peace. However long it takes for us to come to that point depends on so many different things. Finding a good book, a confidant, or professional counselors may be necessary to help you come to terms with your own grief.

Are you grieving the loss of a loved one? The loss of a relationship? The loss of the person you once were? Or the loss of the person your loved one once was? I found hope and comfort in the Bible. Christ met my every need in so many ways.

I pray that you too will find the love of Christ for your life and that you too will find peace as you rest in his everlasting arms. Amen.

_____

_____

_____

_____

_____

_____

_____

A Walk with God

On May 22, 2006, while attending a chaplain's retreat in Oregon, I wrote these words:

"I went for a walk with God today.

"I walked to the edge of the forest and stopped. Trees towered above me. Ahead lay brambles, moss, and fallen trees. I saw no path. In the distance, light streamed through the trees.

"My life feels like this forest. I see no path to guide me. There are many bumps looming ahead that I cannot see. I am drawn to the light. So I wait until I am led to a path. For now I gaze at the light and yearn for its warmth. And I wait for the Lord to lead me in this new journey.

"Looking around, I find a small path that leads through another part of the forest. It takes me to a small clearing where, for a moment, I am engulfed in sunlight. The clouds soon cover the sun, and

MY WILL, GOD'S RESPONSE: GOD'S WILL, MY RESPONSE

the warmth fades. I walk on. The fragrance of the pines fills my nostrils. Carefully watching each step, I press on. Where will the path lead? What is my future? I only know that as I walk, the warmth of God's love will continue to be with me.

"Soon, I am walking on the gravel road. It reminds me that I now walk alone. The road, wider than the path, accentuates the loneliness. Yet again, the sun breaks through the clouds, sending warm rays that fill my being. The forest is quiet. In the quiet, I begin to hear birds chirping. The wind gently rustles the leaves on the trees. A babbling brook brings a calming respite. Under my feet, I hear the crunching of the gravel on the road. The grandeur of God's creation is all around me. Beautiful flowering bushes line the road. The majestic trees stand guard on either side. I am not really walking alone. God walks with me. He fills my life with blessings. I can choose to look at the long, lonely road ahead, or I can choose to stop, listen, smell, and behold the beauty God has placed beside me.

"God went for a walk with me today!"

What brambles are lining your path today? What changes in your path of life must you make? Are you listening for the chirping birds, the babbling brook, or the rustling leaves? Can you see the beautiful flowers, the stately trees, or the majestic mountains? Or is your focus on the bramble bushes and stones that line your path?

Lord, help me to always listen for your voice as we walk together each day. So often I get caught up in the day's activities that I forget to listen for your voice. Please forgive me. Amen.

_____

_____

_____

_____

_____

_____

_____

_____

MY WILL, GOD'S RESPONSE: GOD'S WILL, MY RESPONSE

Traveling

About three months after Ethan died, I took my first vacation alone. This was one of the hardest things for me, and it still is. Ethan and I always traveled together. I didn't know how much I would miss those driving trips. While I was an army wife, I spent a year alone with the children. So being alone at home was not new, but traveling alone was. My first travels took me from Seattle to Omaha for a family reunion, to Sacramento for Philip's wedding, and back to Seattle. These next few lessons are the reflections I wrote on the first leg of that journey in Nebraska for the family reunion.

"Today, I am traveling alone for the first time since the death of my beloved husband, Ethan. I am finding my own way, choosing my own path. I'm really not traveling alone, as God is right here with me in the car I am driving and in the days and months ahead of the life I now lead. How soon we forget that God is always right beside us!

"As I turn the corner, the road I am traveling is flanked on both sides with maple and cottonwood trees. I feel protected, sheltered from the world around me. The comfort that God promises engulfs me; peace and tranquility fill my spirit. The spiritual and emotional road is fearful when I take my eyes off of Jesus. But when I focus on the love of God for me, I can feel his presence and his protection.

"Psalm 36:5–8 speaks of how God's love reaches to the heavens, his faithfulness to the skies, his righteousness is like the mountains, his justice as deep as the ocean, his unfailing love is priceless, his wings provide a refuge in their shadow.

> "Find rest O my soul, in God alone
>
> He alone is my rock and my salvation.
>
> He is my fortress. I will not be shaken."
>
> Psalm 62:5–6

I hold onto this passage for strength and stability for my life.

My heart is filled with the peace of God. He is my rock, my fortress. I do not know where this road will lead. What will I see or encounter along it? Yet I have a map; I know my destination. For now, I take heart in the comfort of the journey.

Lord, as we travel together, may I let you lead me on the path you would have me to go. May you be my light when my way seems dark and dreary. To you I look for strength. Amen.

Are you beginning a new journey in your life? Where are you headed? Is the way plain, or are you struggling to find the correct path? Look to Jesus and find rest in God alone.

_____

_____

_____

_____

_____

_____

_____

_____

MY WILL, GOD'S RESPONSE: GOD'S WILL, MY RESPONSE

Destination

My immediate destination is the family reunion in Chester, Nebraska. The road map shows me that if I carefully follow this highway, I will arrive at the desired city. Road maps are very important when driving in unfamiliar territory. Traveling the road of life also requires a spiritual map.

"Your word is a lamp to my feet and a light to my path" (Psalm 119:105).

Guided by the Word of God each day, each mile is mapped out for us. We can rest assured that whatever the day or mile may bring, God is riding right along with us. He is guiding us to our final destination.

I look forward to seeing dear family members and the celebration and fellowship that we will enjoy at the family reunion. I am thinking of another celebration when I shall meet my loved

MY WILL, GOD'S RESPONSE: GOD'S WILL, MY RESPONSE

ones again at God's forever party. What a joyous time that will be! Jesus said, "In my father's house are many rooms; if it were not so, I would have told you. I am going there to prepare a place for you, I will come back and take you to be with me that you also may be where I am." (John 14:2–3)

My current destination is a temporary one. I will enjoy the weekend and then be gone. My eternal destination is far more important. Where will I spend eternity? My destination is sure because Jesus became a man, lived the perfect life that I cannot, and shed his blood on the cross for the forgiveness of my sins that I might have eternal life.

Do you have assurance of where you will spend eternity? If you do not have a church home where you can get this assurance, pray to God and ask him to send you to the correct church.

Lord, I praise you for your plan of salvation. I thank you that you included everyone when Jesus died on that cross. May my life reflect your love to those whom you place in my path. Amen.

_____

_____

_____

_____

_____

_____

_____

_____

MY WILL, GOD'S RESPONSE: GOD'S WILL, MY RESPONSE

Comfort

I have just crossed from one county into another. Suddenly, the blacktop road, which was gray, has turned into a bright rust color. This is a shocking reminder of how my life changed the day Ethan died. The usual patterns of life have become drastically different. Where do I go from here? What am I to do with my life now?

The hymn writer speaks to my soul. Two verses from "Abide With Me" fill my heart with comfort.

> Swift to its close ebbs out life's little day
>
> Earth's joys grow dim, its glories pass away;
>
> Change and decay in all around I see.
>
> O Thou, who changest not, Abide with me!

I fear no foe, with Thee at hand to bless;

Ills have no weight and tears no bitterness.

Where is death's sting? Where, grave thy victory?

I triumph still if Thou abide with me.[9]

What comfort to know that the never-changing God should care about me when everything around me has changed! We know that life will change. We will experience both joys and sorrow. How will we face sorrow? Do we live with fear and dread of what might happen? God is waiting for us to call upon him to help us through the tough times of life. He is as close as a whispered prayer.

Lord, let me not keep you waiting. I give my life to you. Use it to help someone find rest in you. There is no greater joy than to have peace deep down in one's soul. There is no fear because you are here. Thank you, Lord. Amen.

_____

_____

_____

_____

_____

_____

_____

_____

_____

MY WILL, GOD'S RESPONSE: GOD'S WILL, MY RESPONSE

Vulnerable

Now the road leads me through open territory. There is no protection on either side from nature's elements. The comfort I felt moments ago is gone. I feel vulnerable. Life's turns created change for me. With Ethan at my side, I felt protected, secure. Now, stepping out alone, making a new path, brings vulnerability. But thanks be to God who reaches down where I am and lifts me up.

Psalm 91:15–16 states, "He will call upon me, and I will answer him. I will be with him in trouble; I will deliver him and honor him. With long life will I satisfy him and show him my salvation."

Reading God's Word takes me from feeling lost and unprotected back to comfort. I read in Psalm 119:76: "May your unfailing love be my comfort according to your promise to your servant."

And again in Isaiah 61:1a, 2b-3a: "The Spirit of the Sovereign Lord is on me...to comfort all who morn, and provide for those who grieve in Zion—to bestow on them a crown of beauty instead of ashes, the oil of gladness instead of mourning and a garment of praise instead of a spirit of despair."

So, as I go forward in life, I will have times of vulnerability. How I choose to deal with these is up to me. I can look at all the problems I face and feel despair. Or I can choose to look to God to fill me with the peace he promises, the crown of beauty, a garment of praise.

Are you overwhelmed with trials? Do you feel vulnerable? How are you dealing with these feelings? Where is your focus today?

When I take my eyes off of you, Lord, and life seems to be getting the best of me, forgive me and bring me back to you. Let me again feel your loving arms enfolding me. Let me feel your peace that is beyond all understanding. Let me rest in you. Amen.

MY WILL, GOD'S RESPONSE: GOD'S WILL, MY RESPONSE

Loneliness

My road takes me out into the open countryside. Trees and farmlands stretch for miles. It is a lonely feeling to be away from the towns and homes. Into this lonely feeling God says to me, "I am here with you. You need not feel alone." He fills my lonely space with himself.

Suddenly, I see homes. Some rundown shacks, some new construction. I am not alone. I think of how each day God is bringing old friends to my side. He is adding new people, new experiences, and new activities into my life. I am not who I was four months ago. I am changing. I am God's work in progress.

Thank you, Lord, for all the wonderful friends and family that have been a part of my life for many years. Thank you also for all the new friends I have made these last two years. May I take each new experience, each new activity, as a blessing sent from you. Amen.

Are you lonely or fearful? Has life left you feeling that you are all alone with no one at your side? Have you made an intention of reaching out in friendship? Or do you expect others to reach out to you? Change your focus. Look for the blessings God is waiting to shower upon you as you draw closer to him. Step out in faith and let the Lord be your companion and guide. Rest in him.

_____

_____

_____

_____

_____

_____

_____

_____

O Lord, How Long?

This road I am driving seems very long. How long will it take me to get to my destination? What will happen between here and there? As the hymn writer wrote:

> Trust and obey, Trust and obey,
>
> for there's no better way to be happy in Jesus
>
> than to trust and obey.[10]

Soon my travels bring me safely to my destination. At each curve in the road, each intersection, I am guided by road signs.

My travel continues to my heavenly destination. I am still experiencing the curves in the road, sometimes the detours, and always the intersections where I must choose which way to go. When I get off on the wrong road, God brings me back to the correct one. With my eyes on him, following his road map found in the Bible, I will one day enjoy the feast in heaven prepared for all those who love him.

Until that day, I will continue to live for God. I will not be living the life he wants. I can never be perfect. But thanks to Jesus who was perfect for me, I will go on forgiven and blessed.

What crossroads are you faced with in your life today? How will your choice affect your life? Have you given these choices to the Lord so that he can help you make good decisions?

May I always keep my eyes on Jesus and the blessings he bestows. May my life be a living sacrifice for him. Amen.

_____

_____

_____

_____

_____

_____

_____

_____

God's Will: My Response

Ethan had so wanted to be able to participate in the wedding ceremony of Philip and Christina in August. In Ethan's memory, a picture of him was placed in the front of the church together with a candle, which I lit. Before he died, Ethan wrote a blessing for them. I read that blessing as a part of the service. It wasn't how we had planned it, but it was God's plan.

It has now been over two years since Ethan's death. In that time, I have flown to visit the boys several times, to LWML conventions, and to family reunions. I continue as a board member for Lutheran Ministry Services Northwest, the organization for which Ethan worked. I have been available to drive senior citizens to doctors in Seattle. I have joined the Chancel Choir at church and have become a member of the prayer group.

I have prepared and have led an LWML district retreat. I have also gone back to work on a limited schedule. I dreamt I was talking to Ethan the other night. He had asked me how I was doing. I told him that what I missed the most were our driving trips around the country. He seemed happy. I know that Ethan is no longer suffering and is now in the loving arms of the Savior. He is at peace. That knowledge has given me real peace.

One day, I asked God why he would take Ethan so young. His answer was that he had work for me to do that I would not or could not do while Ethan was alive. God has a plan for my life. I feel that this book is a part of that plan. Where he leads from here, I do not know. I feel that there is still work for me to accomplish. If I am faithful to listen, he will reveal it at the right time.

What work does God have for you to accomplish? Think about your passions. How can you use these gifts in ministry to others?

Lord, you give us breath. You have numbered our days. You created a path for us to walk. Sometimes we do not like the path we are on and want another one. Some days we are on the wrong path because of our own choosing. Lord, I ask not that you bless the path I choose, but that I would choose the path that you have already blessed. Amen.

_____

_____

_____

_____

_____

_____

_____

_____

MY WILL, GOD'S RESPONSE: GOD'S WILL, MY RESPONSE

God's Plan for Our Tomorrows

Look at your life and especially at events you thought were tragic. Did God have a blessing within that tragedy? Have you grown in your faith or have you become bitter? Turn your hurts over to Jesus and ask him to show you his blessings. They are all around us.

God does not always answer our prayers as we want. Sometimes he has a better plan for our lives and the spreading of his kingdom. Had circumstances been different, I would never have written this book.

> "For my thoughts are not your thoughts,
> neither are your ways my ways,"
> declares the Lord. "As the heavens are
> higher than the earth, so are my ways
> higher than your ways and my thoughts

MY WILL, GOD'S RESPONSE: GOD'S WILL, MY RESPONSE

than your thoughts. As the rain and the snow come down from heaven, and do not return to it without watering the earth and making it bud and flourish, so that it yields seed for the sower and bread for the eater, so is my word that goes out from my mouth: It will not return to me empty, but will accomplish what I desire and achieve the purpose for which I sent it."

Isaiah 55:8–11

May you be blessed for having walked this journey with me. I pray you have been strengthened in your life by the lessons I learned and have shared in this book.

_____

_____

_____

_____

_____

_____

To God be the glory!

References

Photo of Chaplain Ethan Voges by Olan Mills is used by permission.

"In the Garden" - Public Domain

"His Eye Is on the Sparrow" - Public Domain

Great Is Thy Faithfulness. Copyright 1923. Renewal 1951 extended by Hope Publishing Co., Carol Stream, IL 60188. All rights reserved. Used by permission.

"Guide Me O Thou Great Redeemer" - Public Domain

Because He Lives. Copyright 1971 by Bill Gaither. All rights reserved. International copyright secured. Used by permission.

"On Eagles Wings." Copyright OCP Publications. All rights reserved. Used by permission.

"Amazing Grace" - Public Domain

"It Is No Secret." Copyright 1950 by Stuart Hamblen. All rights reserved. Used by permission from Hamblen Music.

"Abide With Me" and "Trust and Obey" - Public Domain

Bible passages are from the New International Version, except for Psalm 63, which is from *God's Word* translation, Word Publishing.

Endnotes

1   *In the Garden* by C. Austin Mills—Public
domain

2   *His Eye is on the Sparrow* by Mrs. C.D.
Martin—Public Domain

3   *Great Is Thy Faithfulness* by Thomas
O. Chisholm © 1923. Ren. 1951 Hope
Publishing Co., Carol Stream, IL 60188.
All rights reserved. Used by permission.
Reprinted under license #P2009-174

4   *Guide Me O Thou Great Redeemer* by William
Williams—Public Domain

5   *BECAUSE HE LIVES* Words by William J. and
Gloria Gaither. Music by William J. Gaither.
Copyright © 1971 William J. Gaither, Inc.
All rights controlled by Gaither Copyright
Management. Used by permission.

6 *On Eagle's Wings* © 1979, Jan Michael Joncas, Published by OCP, 5526 NE Hassalo, Portland, OR 97213 All rights reserved. Used with permission.

7 *Amazing Grace* by John Newton—Public Domain

8 *It is No Secret* by Stuart Hamblen © 1950 Hamblen Music. All rights reserved. Used by permission.

9 *Abide With Me* by Henry Flyte—Public Domain

10 *Trust and Obey* by James H. Sammis—Public Domain

Other references

e|LIVE

---

listen|imagine|view|experience

AUDIO BOOK DOWNLOAD INCLUDED WITH THIS BOOK!

In your hands you hold a complete digital entertainment package. Besides purchasing the paper version of this book, this book includes a free download of the audio version of this book. Simply use the code listed below when visiting our website. Once downloaded to your computer, you can listen to the book through your computer's speakers, burn it to an audio CD or save the file to your portable music device (such as Apple's popular iPod) and listen on the go!

How to get your free audio book digital download:

1. Visit www.tatepublishing.com and click on the e|LIVE logo on the home page.
2. Enter the following coupon code:
   b38a-cea6-47fb-5e7c-5281-bab5-ac91-8538
3. Download the audio book from your e|LIVE digital locker and begin enjoying your new digital entertainment package today!